amy butler's
midwest modern

a fresh design spirit for the modern lifestyle

Published in 2007 by Stewart, Tabori & Chang
An imprint of Harry N. Abrams, Inc.

Library of Congress Cataloging-in-Publication Data

Butler, Amy.
Amy Butler's midwest modern : a fresh design spirit for the modern lifestyle / text & style by Amy Butler ; photography & design by David Butler.
p. cm.
  ISBN 978-1-58479-581-0 (hardcover with jacket)
 I. Butler, Amy. 2. Lifestyles. 3. Creative ability. I. Butler, David. II. Title. III. Title: Midwest modern.

NK2004.3.B88.A35 2007
747–dc22   2006100282

Editor: Dervla Kelly
Designer: David Butler
Production Manager: Jacquie Poirier

The text of this book was composed in Century and Mrs. Eaves fonts.

Printed and bound in China
10 9 8 7 6 5 4 3 2 1

HNA
harry n. abrams, inc.
a subsidiary of La Martinière Groupe

115 West 18th Street
New York, NY 10011
www.hnabooks.com

This book is dedicated to my husband David for helping me realize my dreams.

INTRODUCTION   10

1. MEET AMY   14
PERSONAL INTRODUCTION TO MY LIFE

2. PASSIVE SPACES   20
DESIGN AND STYLE FOR AREAS OF RELAXATION AND DREAMING
LIVING ROOM, BED & BATH, MUSIC AND MEDITATION SPOTS

3. ACTIVE SPACES   80
KEEPING IT TOGETHER AT WORK AND PLAY!
CREATIVE STUDIO SPACE, KITCHEN AND DINING

4. BODY AS CANVAS   120
FASHION AND ACCESSORIZING WITH PERSONAL VOICE
EASY AND KINETIC IDEAS COMBINING VINTAGE & NEW

5. NATURAL HIGHLIGHTS   180
GARDENS AND NATURE SKETCHBOOKS TO INSPIRE DESIGN
ARTISTIC AND INSPIRATIONAL SPACES AND SPECIMENS

6. GYPSY CARAVAN   206
GETTING AWAY FROM IT ALL WITH STYLE ON THE ROAD
FINDING INSPIRATION AT THE FLEA MARKET
GYPSY PICNICS, AND A SIMPLE LAKESIDE R&R

EPILOGUE   220

RESOURCE GUIDE   222

acknowledgments

THE BEST PART OF ANY CREATIVE VENTURE IS THE COLLABORATION WITH OTHERS. AN ARTISTIC PROJECT IN ANY FORM UNITES IDEAS AND BRINGS OUT TALENTS THAT MIGHT OTHERWISE LIE DORMANT. THANKS TO EVERYONE WHO HELPED IN THE MAKING OF THIS BOOK FOR YOUR UNWAVERING SUPPORT AND CONTINUAL INSPIRATION. CLEARLY, IT COULD NOT HAPPEN WITHOUT THE HANDS OF MANY.

THANKS TO MY HUSBAND DAVID FOR SHARING NOT ONLY HIS ARTISTIC EYE, BUT ALSO HIS HEART AND MIND FOR THE LAST 20 YEARS. TO DIANE CAPACI, DIANNE BARCUS, AND KIM VENTURA FOR BEING THE CONSTANT CREATIVE MACHINERY BEHIND OUR BUSINESS AND OUR LIVES. TO JAKE REDINGER FOR BEING THE SAIL TO OUR "DESIGN SHIP." TO ALL OF THE SEAMSTRESSES IN OUR COMMUNITY WHO KEEP THE ENERGY HIGH AND THE SPIRITS HIGHER. TO CAROLINE AND MARC FOR SEEING BEYOND THE CREATIVE WORK TO THE VERY IDEA ITSELF. TO DERVLA AND EVERYONE AT STC FOR HELPING TO TRANSLATE MY THOUGHTS AND ENERGY INTO A FOCUSED EFFORT (NO SMALL TASK) AND FOR BELIEVING IN ME. TO MY FAMILY AND DAVID'S FAMILY FOR THEIR CONSTANT LOVE. AND TO MY FRIENDS WHO ALWAYS SUPPORT AND LOVE ME FOR WHO I AM.

INTRODUCTION

I THINK THAT IN EVERYTHING WE DO, IN EVERY STYLE OF LIFE, THERE IS ART TO BE FOUND. NOT JUST IN THE STUDIOS OF TALENTED ARTISTS, BUT IN THE GARDENS, HOMES, RELATIONSHIPS, SPIRITS, VOICES, AND FASHIONS OF PEOPLE YOU SEE EVERY DAY.

LIFE & ART

Life itself is artistic. The profound beauty of nature, creatures, motion, stillness, work, communication, spaces, emotions, and even gravity inspires us all. For me, it's all about staying attuned to that very idea. It's easy to lose sight of this when daily life is comprised of important (and not-so-important) hurdles that need focus. But there's nothing to say this feeling can't stay somewhere in the back of your mind—and that's balance.

Of course, I'm simply a designer. This philosophy might seem grandiose, but it's how I maintain balance in my own life, and how I find my aesthetic voice. When I create a new design for a fabric, I'm not trying to make the world more beautiful; I'm only creating something I enjoy, using the visual cues of my surroundings. And if my surroundings don't inspire me, I set about the task of changing them— either by reinventing them, or by traveling to find new ideas.

In that way, I try to lead a kinetic and flexible life. That's why this book is very exciting for me. On the outside, I'm a quiet person. (Don't ask my husband or my friends to retort, they will lie to you). I express myself through my art and design. I say this because when you see my work, you might think I'm a bit of an extrovert. You might not put the art with the person. But I'm inwardly optimistic and hopeful and use art as a means to show it. I see the distinct connection between all the different aspects of a person's life as contributing to their overall artistic voice. That's why this book covers fashion, home, garden, and even a bit of travel. Textures, colors, fragrances, sounds, and even tastes are explored as well. If this book is truly to be an insight into my inspirations, well, it has a big job to do.

SURROUNDINGS

I would be happiest if, after perusing this book, you felt inspired by your own style and surroundings, or felt the impetus to create that feeling for yourself. I began designing sewing patterns because I wanted to create my own style of handbags. I found that even though they were my designs, when other people made them, they would instill their own sensibilities—in fabrics, pins, and colors—to make their own style. The ideas generated in this book are for your interpretation—a starting point for your personal creativity.

It's not about money or talent. It's about creativity and love. I put my personality into everything I do, and that makes it both exciting and intimate. When I put on my clothing in the morning, or design fabrics, or choose colors for a room, I want it to be a reflection of the confident and optimistic person I aspire to be. That is why home decor and fashion are so much more than fluff and pomp. They are the calling cards to our personalities. The very act of participating in your personal appearance and the creation of your surroundings defines how you see yourself.

Objects, colors, patterns, smells, and textures can transcend the surroundings you live in. My husband fancies himself a Midwestern surfer. Our home does much to perpetuate this fantasy, despite our Ohio location. To look at the exterior of our house—the 12-foot banana trees, the cypress, the mid-century modern styling—you would think we live in the hills of Southern California. He leaves his skateboards lying about the house, evoking images from Australian home magazines; the open floor plan and natural finishes of warm wood and stone perpetuate his dream. We spend our summers mostly barefoot inside, and we open every window and door to let in the fragrances of pine and cut grass. It's easy to be creative in such a setting. Our surroundings inspire us.

MIDWEST MODERN

I don't follow trends per se. Like everyone else, I do enjoy the ebb and flow of the fashion tide. But I feel that trends cannot keep up with my ever-changing moods. I keep my home, fashion, and life kinetic so that I can continually breathe new life into them. In the end, style is only the whim of the day, or week, or however long it suits our fancy. We place great value on what we consider "timeless style," but in 200 years, who will really know? Or care? I can't think of one designer from colonial America.

The term "Midwest Modern" has been used to describe my work. I think it's very appropriate—so much so, in fact, that I use it as my brand tagline. It may suggest a humorous poke at either coast, but that's not the intention. It's merely a way to call attention to our beautiful heartland, and to project confidence in our ability to create our own artistic voices outside of the larger stream of fashion. Of course, in today's increasingly globalized world, it's becoming more and more difficult to either hide from—or reinvent—mass consumer culture. Let's just say we Midwesterners choose what works, and only what works, and leave the rest behind. That's why we're the ultimate test market, and why merchants and marketers proclaim, "If it doesn't play in the heartland, it won't play."

I consider "Midwest" as an honest, approachable, easy style of personal vision. "Modern" is taking that style and applying it to today's world. Softening technology while embracing it. Honoring vintage design while reinventing it. The best experiences in life are ones that are exciting and new, while still feeling familiar and comfortable—that's Midwest Modern.

TAKING CARE

This book touts design, art, and ideas to jump-start your creative spark. It also might give you a sense of my passion for recycling, reusing, and reducing. This is part and parcel of everything we do at my studio, and of how I try to lead my life—only buying what I need, buying locally when I can, and choosing quality over quantity. This philosophy is inherent in the ideas laid out here: reusing vintage clothing and furnishings, making your own cool home and fashion items, gardening organically to help sustain your ecosystem, and simply—well, *living* simply.

Enlightened decision-making is key to our business at the studio as well. We work to sustain a cottage industry of local seamstresses, engage in fundraisers for our women's shelter and food bank, and support the area's animal shelters. Your community supports you, whether you see it or not, and so it's vital to work to maintain a healthy, viable relationship with it. This is essential to the optimistic vision that inspires me, and it is dear to my heart. You cannot create entirely for yourself; you must engage in the world that surrounds you. This idea may not be visible in the smiling faces, fun patterns, or soothing places in this book, but it's woven into the making of it all.

meet amy

As a young girl, I excelled at drawing mushrooms, frogs, and flowers. It was, after all, the 70s.

I moved into owls later, and then, feeling confident, into horses. This might be the key to my style. If my work feels "groovy" at times, it's because it is. It's groovy because I allow myself to think the way I did as a little girl, to see what I want to see, and to draw what I wish to draw. If anything, I'm less hindered now, because as a child I tied myself to the icons of the times. Almost all young girls were drawing the same things, trying to evoke their drawing mastery and develop their own style.

I still approach design with a mixture of curiosity, spontaneity, and a genuine love of creating. I worked hard in art school to hone my skill without losing a sense of intrigue and passion—exploring shapes, colors, textures, and style. Surface design and fashion became my obsession. I would draw enormously tall women with impossible necks and on them I would create lavish, layered clothing. Within those layers, I would doodle in signature florals, patterns, stripes, and modern geometrics. I found that the passionate creation of the print outweighed my love of the clothing. I focused my efforts on the design of pattern. (Skeptics beware: I can still draw a frog if cornered.)

Today I'm sitting in the studio working on my newest line of fabrics, surrounded by a vast array of markers, color swatches, drawing pads, and Post-it notes (my life is arranged with Post-it notes). Birdie, the little black cat you'll see plenty of in this book, is pulling yet another skein of yarn out of my cubby. *I guess I won't be knitting with that one.* It reminds me to pack my knitting supplies for the upcoming vacation getaway with our friends later this month—a caravan to some flea markets, then a lakeside retreat. I can feel the cool breeze now. I have the windows wide open, and I can see that the deer have been eating my oak leaf hydrangea—again.

When I got up this morning, it was foggy out. I went out to the deck and meditated, did a few stretches, and checked on the progress of the single Night-Blooming Cereus blossom that's wrapped around the deck railing. Our house sits perched on the side of a steep hill overlooking the valley that envelops our town. Way up to the left you can see college dorms on the hill, and out in front is the village golf course, developed in the 1920s, that holds a gorgeous array of specimen trees. I was going to go for a walk but David, my husband, got me to have a cup of coffee on the porch—we call it procrastination alley. When we do this, or when we do go for walks, it's the time we can clear our heads and make plans for the day or week ahead.

We're working on a new line of finished goods—bags and such—and I have to meet with my team this morning. We have to coordinate the Web store, take photos of samples before they go back to the vendor, choose zippers, detail finished seams, conference-call with the manufacturer, and then proofread the latest sewing patterns. Three of the local women who sew for us will be coming in soon to pick up work, so we have to choose fabrics. And then maybe have lunch. It's crazy at times, but always new and exciting. Without the people I work with, I wouldn't last an hour!

I've just picked the three color palettes for my new fabrics, and I'm putting together image boards of inspiration. I love to develop the name of the line, and the story. Usually David helps me. We develop names and bounce them off each other, then create a story, or maybe a place, that becomes the inspiration for the collection. It breathes romance into the line—which helps bring it to life. It's a good way to look at your business as well, to help clarify your goals and create an aesthetic. Build a story around it, and follow it through.

CLOCKWISE: Sketches for a quilt design and an ad from the Lotus line of fabrics. • Birdie on the verge of getting into my yarn. • Answering emails (a major part of my work!) at my vintage farm table desk.

My scattered piles of sketches—for quilts, patterns, clothing, bags—lie in a heap on my desk. This is what happens when the ideas and the deadlines come fast and furious. No matter. I'm still learning the cadence of my workload, and as soon as I do, it changes. We have a mantra: WORK IS CHAOS. And if you understand that, every ounce of forward momentum makes you feel like you're in complete control. Pace and balance. Moderation in all things. Taking our work and our art seriously, but not ourselves. After all, we're still an art studio. If we fail in some way, nobody dies. Another mantra that we work hard to follow is this: IMPATIENCE IS SELF-IMPORTANCE. There is time for everyone, and everyone is important.

Most important in my world is the company I keep. My friends, family, and pets. They are the reason I enjoy my studio and my life as an artist, and they are the best part of stepping away from that world. What I do is not as important as whom I love. I'll drop it all in order to be with someone who needs me. No career is worth losing our connection as people, and no art is more important than the people who make it (or for whom it's made). Maybe I am still "groovy." I believe in Love. I believe we can inspire change in each other, and in the world. I believe that we can help those around us to become happier people, even in the little things, like how we enjoy our clothes or our homes. These things give us confidence, and help us define our place. After all, if we can't find creative fire, love, passion, excitement, and pure joy in the little everyday things, where will we find it?

–Amy

CLOCKWISE: Two fashion drawings from my art school portfolio—note the long necks. • David and I, relieved that we've successfully put up another fun trade show booth! • Focused intent (or maybe confusion) while working on one of my dress patterns. • Family portraits from my studio shelf—my mother as a little girl and my grandmother (who taught me to sew) on one of her fishing expeditions in the 1950s. • A bowl of my tags ready to be sewn into finished pieces. • Matching color chips for buttons.

passive spaces

In creating this book, I felt it important to really look at my surroundings honestly. They break down into the places I go to relax and regroup, and the places I work.

Now, it might seem funny that I start with the passive spaces (where I unwind), since you're likely reading this because you enjoy my work. Well, the calm, soothing places where I relax are also my design laboratory. They are kinetic and flexible spaces that can change on a whim, and usually do change at the release of a new line of my fabric. We slipcover vintage chairs, make or recover floor cushions, and always have an array of my pillows scattered about. One thing you will notice is that I do not saturate my living areas with pattern or bright color. That way the injection of new and changing patterns and colors doesn't collide with a fussy or complicated room. It gives me a clean canvas on which to try new ideas without having to repaint (or reupholster).

Organic is a word that comes to mind when people visit our house. Not only is there a very natural feel to the finishes and decor, but you also get a sense that we didn't design it all at once. Rather, we let the home develop over time, to grow into the design. David and I have written other books and created magazine stories on interior design, and we can tell you that even for experienced professionals, there is no point in rushing the process. An end result is not necessarily the goal. A space that allows you to constantly evolve it, change it, and experiment with it is key to my artistic life. We have a modern-style living space, but within it we strive to combine great textures and forms. Mid-century design mingles with primitive, even folk, vernaculars. We hide technology away the best we can, unless it is artistic in itself.

Passive spaces in my world are comprised of the living rooms, bedrooms, and bath. These are the spaces I retire to at the end of the day when the phones have stopped ringing, the fabric has stopped flying, and the studio is at rest. They are where I see how the fruits of my creative labor can be applied in real life, and not just as swatches on my wall. I love to relax with them, combine them with the styles of other designers, and watch the cats indiscriminately groom themselves all over my latest creations.

THE BiG Room

OUR FRIENDS HAVE DUBBED OUR HOME THE TREE HOUSE. THE WAY OUR HOME IS SITUATED ON A STEEP HILL, WE SIT ABOVE THE TREE LINE, WHICH AFFORDS STUNNING VIEWS OF THE TOWN VALLEY. OUR LIVING SPACES ARE CONJOINED AND FREE OF WALLS. ONE SIDE IS DIVIDED FROM THE OTHER BY A LARGE FIREPLACE. THE FIRST SPACE WE CALL THE BIG ROOM. IT'S WHERE WE ENTERTAIN AND EXPERIMENT WITH NEW DESIGNS. WE CAN CLEAR ALL OF THE FURNITURE OUT OF THE ROOM AND BUILD MY TRADE-SHOW BOOTH IN IT (THUS OUR PRIZED PASSIVE SPACE IS ANNEXED TO THE ACTIVE).

ABOVE AND RIGHT: In the forefront are floor cushions that we made in the studio with my fabrics and foam. (There's a brief "How-To" on page 34) • Modern couches are adorned with some of my favorite wool pillows from other amazing designers. • The room faces north with views directly into the higher elevations of the trees which affords great bird watching from our deck dining area just visible in the background. • Mid-century tables and accents tie into the primitive furniture and floors with color, texture, and pattern. • We've dubbed the large cupboard the "Cherry Monster" because it's over seven feet tall, and does not come apart. We've moved it from three different homes.

LEFT PAGE - CLOCKWISE: A reverse view of the Big Room as seen from the front door. You can plainly see the massive stone fireplace that passes through to the other side. • An amazing pastel rendering by our friend Chi Kit hangs above a mid-century armchair. The elephant ear leaf is a cutting from one of our potted giants. • A detail of the wool pillows catches a ray from the skylights above. • Vintage vases and flora of the moment!

ABOVE: Our musical influences are sprinkled throughout. The iPod has revolutionized our lifestyle by making it easy to bring music any-where. • David's CBGB poster sits behind his rare 1936 aluminum bicycle. His passion for bikes has grown on me (and taken over the garage).

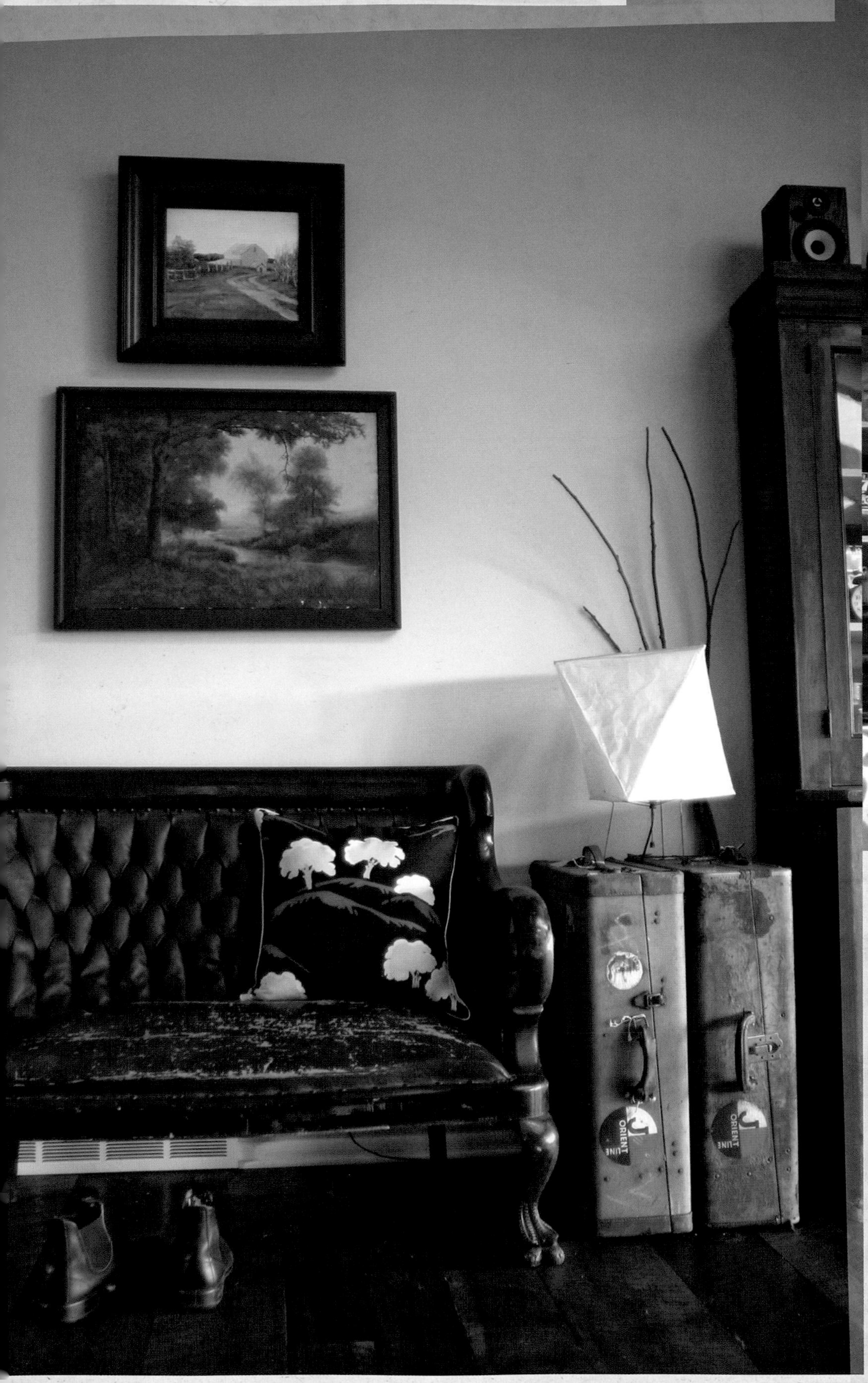
KHJ.9482
ORIENT LINE
ORIENT LINE

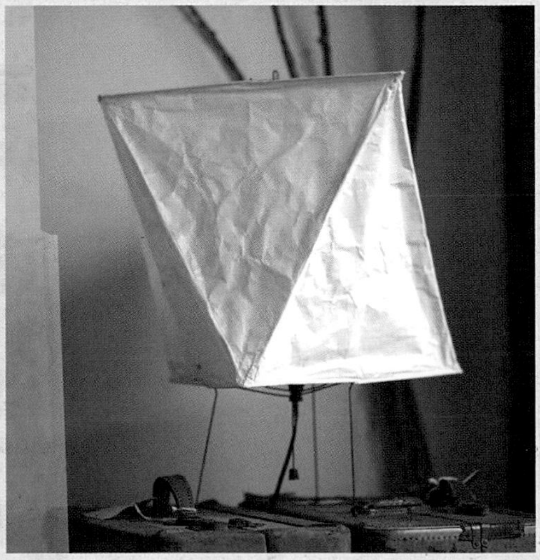

LEFT PAGE: Sometimes modern isn't a design cue, but simply the way you live! These vintage finds are from all over the Midwest including the 1970s Noguchi paper lamp we found in MIchigan. It's age gave it a great hue and wrinkled texture that you can't get with a new one. • A great way to tie together a multitude of paintings in odd frames is to create your own consistency by painting all of the frames the same color. We picked out a tone that reflected the dark accents in the room and still worked with the art. • ABOVE: You can find the inspiration for the green wall color sprinkled throughout the space including the accents in this little plaster bird and 1970s mod McCoy pottery.

At first glance our home seems very simple and ordered. But we temper the style with an unwavering passion for romantic collections. We keep them in the big cherry cupboard behind glass and pull from our collections to accent our home. • None of it is particularly expensive or noteworthy aside from the watercolor painting my friend Nora made for me while on a houseboat vacation together. They're simply fond collections of ephemera and natural discoveries from years of scouring flea markets, wooded trails, and antique shops. It all works together in varying shades of ivory, green, brown, and black.

FLOWERS

CUT FLOWERS ARE ALWAYS A LUXURY. I TRY TO HAVE THEM IN THE HOUSE WHENEVER I CAN. OF COURSE THEY ARE THE MAJOR INSPIRATION FOR MY FABRIC PRINTS AND SO I LOVE TO EXPERIMENT WITH DIFFERENT VARIETIES AND CUTTINGS FROM MY GARDENS.

HERE ARE A FEW QUICK TIPS ON KEEPING CUT FLOWERS FRESHER, LONGER:

LOOK FOR FLOWERS THAT ARE JUST STARTING TO OPEN AND AVOID FLOWERS THAT HAVE BEEN STANDING IN THE HOT SUN OR EXPOSED TO POLLUTION.

MAKE SURE YOUR VASES ARE REALLY CLEAN. BACTERIA CAN BLOCK WATER ABSORPTION. CLEAN WATER IS ESSENTIAL SO CHANGE THE WATER IN THE VASE DAILY OR USE A FLORAL PRESERVATIVE.

CUT OFF A COUPLE OF INCHES OF STEM WITH SHARP SHEARS AND REMOVE ANY LEAVES THAT TRAIL IN THE VASE WATER AS THEY WILL ROT QUICKLY AND POLLUTE. DON'T CRUSH THE STEMS—THE DAMAGED TISSUE WILL NOT ABSORB WATER WELL.

LEFT TO RIGHT: Nothing beats the fragrance of Lilies. Buy and cut them as they are just opening. Be careful of the dark pollen as it will stain! Use tape to pull it off cloth or skin (don't rub it). If something does stain, set it out in the full sun and it will fade. • These Bells of Ireland have a great texture that looks wonderful in a tall, architextural vase. • My Gothic Rose fabric, inspiration clearly evident! • Sunshine Protea has the most amazingly rich colors—from the deep magenta tips to the creamy centers, down to the deep olive stems.

FLOOR cushions

Even if you're a novice seamstress, you might enjoy these

Fairly simple how-to's

FINISH SIZE: 35" X 35" X 12"

YOU'LL NEED:

3 YARDS OF COTTON FABRIC FOR THE COVER
2 PIECES OF 35 X 35 X 6" NU-FOAM (BY FAIRFIELD)
1 60 X 95" PIECE OF POLYESTER BATTING
ELMER'S WHITE GLUE AND STRONG SPRAY GLUE

-CUT TWO 35 X 35" PIECES OF 6" THICK FOAM
-CUT ONE 60 X 95" PIECE OF POLYESTER BATTING
-CUT ONE 36 X 95" PIECE OF COTTON FABRIC, FOR MAIN PANEL
-CUT TWO 13 X 36" PIECES OF COTTON FABRIC, FOR END PANELS

1. SPREAD ELMER'S GLUE GENEROUSLY ON THE TOP OF ONE OF THE FOAM PIECES. STACK THE OTHER PIECE ON TOP AND LET THEM DRY.

2. NEXT, SPRAY THE FOAM WITH A HEAVY-DUTY SPRAY GLUE. WRAP THE BATTING AROUND THE FOAM, CUTTING OFF THE EXCESS BATTING IN THE CORNERS. SET ASIDE.

3. USING A STAY STITCH AND A ½" SEAM ALLOWANCE, SEW DOWN BOTH LONG, RAW EDGES OF THE COTTON FABRIC MAIN PANEL.

4. ON THE LONG EDGE OF THE MAIN PANEL, STARTING AT ONE END, MEASURE AND SNIP (WITH SCISSORS) INTO THE STAY STITCH SEAM ALLOWANCE AT THE FOLLOWING INTERVALS: 35½", 47½", 82½".

5. ON THE OPPOSITE SIDE OF THE MAIN PANEL, STARTING AT THE SAME END, MEASURE AND SNIP INTO THE STAY STITCH SEAM ALLOWANCE AT THE SAME INTERVALS AS IN STEP 4.

6. WITH RIGHT SIDES TOGETHER, PLACE THE MAIN PANEL ON TOP OF THE 36" EDGE OF ONE OF THE END PANELS MATCHING THE RAW EDGES (THE END PANEL WILL EXTEND ½" PAST THE FIRST CLIP). STARTING ½" IN FROM THE 12" SIDE EDGE, SEW A ½" SEAM ALONG THE RAW EDGES, STOPPING AT THE FIRST SNIP, AND BACKSTITCHING AT EACH END.

7. TURN THE MAIN PANEL AT THE FIRST SNIP, LINING UP THE RAW EDGE WITH THE 13" SIDE OF THE END PANEL. SEW A ½" SEAM FROM THE FIRST SNIP, STOPPING AT THE SECOND SNIP, AND BACKSTITCHING AT EACH END.

8. TURN THE MAIN PANEL AT THE SECOND SNIP AND REPEAT THE PROCESS TO STITCH ALONG ALL 4 SIDES OF THE END PANEL.

9. WITH RIGHT SIDES TOGETHER, MATCH UP THE SHORT ENDS OF THE MAIN PANEL. SEW A ½" SEAM, STARTING AND STOPPING ½" FROM EACH END, AND BACKSTITCHING AT EACH END.

10. ON THE OTHER EDGE WITH THE STAY STITCHING, REPEAT STEPS 6-8 TO ATTACH ONE LONG SIDE OF THE OTHER END PANEL TO THE MAIN PANEL.

11. TURN THE COVER RIGHT SIDE OUT, USING A TURNING TOOL TO PUSH OUT EACH OF THE CORNERS, AND PRESS.

12. SLIP THE COVER OVER THE FOAM, PLACING THE SEAMS ALONG THE EDGES OF THE FOAM. FOLD THE END PANEL OVER THE EXPOSED END OF THE FOAM.

13. FOLD THE FABRIC UNDER ½" ON ALL 3 RAW EDGES AND PIN IN PLACE. USING A SLIPSTITCH, CLOSE EDGES ON THE 3 SIDES BY HAND.

envelope pillows

You'll need:
½ yard of cotton fabric for front and back of the pillow
16 x 16" pillow form

- Cut one 17 x 17" piece of fabric for the Front Panel
- Cut two 11 1/2 x 17" pieces of fabric for the Back Panels

1. On both Back Panel pieces, fold and press a ½" seam (toward the WRONG side) on one 17" raw edge. Fold the edges over another ½" and press again. Edge stitch across the inner folded edges on both Back Panel pieces.

2. Overlap the 2 finished edges on the Back Panels by 4" (both pieces should have WRONG sides facing up) and pin the raw edges in place. leave an opening where the seam edges overlap. Attach the 2 Back Panels by machine-basting a ½" seam across both raw edges.

3. Place the Front and Back Panel RIGHT sides together, matching up the raw edges and pinning them in place. Sew a ½" seam around the raw edges of the perimeter of the pillow, backstitching at each end.

4. Finish the seam allowances by serging or using a zigzag stitch around the raw edges.

5. Turn the pillow cover RIGHT side out, using a turning tool to push out the corners. Press.

6. Insert the pillow form through the slit left in the back of the cover.

nature study

Adjacent to the Big Room, we have a sitting area we call the Nature Study. Spending so much time in the garden and woods affords us a great number of hunting and gathering finds. It's a place to relax in the sun and enjoy tactile discoveries, a good book, artwork by our friends, and amiable company.

CLOCKWISE: The nature study affords great southern light, and a perfect view of our courtyard gardens. It's important for us to have a kinetic environment where we can study and display our finds. We really have a "catch and release" program with rocks, leaves, shells, plants, and branches. In order to keep it from cluttering up, we'll study a piece for a while, and then take it back outside. Of course we never bring in anything living. The cats would go crazy! • The couch is a vintage two-piece we had recovered and the chairs are Mid-century Bertoia finds. David cut down the old kitchen table to function at coffee table height. • Julio the cat is particularly drawn to the nature study. Likely it's the abundant sunshine and the wild lion feeling he gets hanging out under the eucalyptus. • Sometimes the simplest patterns are the most organic. If you study hard, you can find the dot pattern revealed in almost every aspect of nature.

Polytrichum commune / Haarmoos

Lehrmittelverlag Hagemann,
in Arbeitsgemeinschaft mit Frommann & Morian

These vintage botanical studies are a great source of inspiration. I love to picture the silhouettes in a wonderful repeat pattern! • Details of our nature table reflect the simple pleasures and interesting textures to be found on a walk in the woods.

masculine & feminine

{ FINDING BALANCE, ESPECIALLY WITH YOUR HUSBAND }

INSPIRATION HITS DAVID AND I WITH THE SAME VIGOR, BUT FROM DIFFERENT SOURCES. I KNOW I'M LUCKY THAT HE DOESN'T FEEL THE COMPULSION TO HANG POSTERS OF HIS FAVORITE SPORTS TEAMS IN THE LIVING ROOM. SO WE'VE STRUCK A BALANCE OF DESIGN THAT STAYS TRUE TO OUR COLLECTIVE VISION, BUT TAKES INTO CONSIDERATION INDIVIDUAL PASSIONS. WE'VE SET A BASIC STRUCTURE OF DESIGN THAT IS WARM, INVITING, AND TACTILE — ARTISTIC BUT NOT SHOWY. AND MAYBE MOST IMPORTANTLY WE'VE VOWED THAT CHANGE IS GOOD, INEVITABLE, AND FUN! SO EVEN IF HE'S NOT CRAZY ABOUT AN IDEA, CHANCES ARE IT WILL CHANGE IN DUE TIME. PAINT COLORS CAN CHANGE IN A WEEKEND, PILLOWS AND SLIPCOVERS TOO.
WE SEE OUR HOME AS A LIVING, BREATHING SPACE FULL OF IDEAS, MOTION, AND LOVE. IT'S NOT A SHOWROOM, OR A MUSEUM. WE WANT IT TO HONOR VISITORS WITH INSPIRATION AND WARMTH, AND MAYBE TELL THEM A LITTLE BIT ABOUT WHO WE ARE. WE EACH HAVE A VOICE IN IT.

ABOVE: David's nature study stick collection meets my 1920s opalescent glass chandelier.
Strikingly similar colors but totally different textures. His was cheaper.

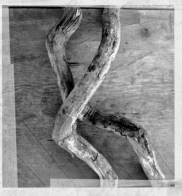

COLLECTING NATURE

Here are some images that show the beauty in both natural objects and objects made to honor natural forms. You can see why I love to collect them. They give me great design ideas and inspiration for color and pattern.

If it's not possible to take something along, a great photograph will always do. And when it comes to shells and other parts of living creatures, it's important not to "live harvest" for a trinket.

43

INDOOR POTTED PLANTS

Living in the midwest presents both challenges and benefits to growing plants. The benefits being dramatic seasonal changes provide dramatic changes in color and an amazing rebirth every spring. The downside is winter. We move plants inside and out often. Especially in the transitional times of late spring when we're anxious to get the potted plants back out into the fresh air. It's not too hard to maintain indoor potted plants, and it's well worth it. Here's a few very basic tips to follow:

Keep plants off heat registers and out of direct hot air paths that can quickly dry out pots— especially in the winter when the air itself is much drier.

Be sure to put plants where the most beneficial levels of light can be found. For many of our tropical plants, we move them into the basement with grow lights and keep them under watch.

Use natural insecticidal soaps to keep white flies and other invaders from sucking the life out of your plants. These soaps also help to keep pets from chewing on tender leaves but won't harm them.

Most plants respond well to trimming. Dead-heading flower blooms is also important to keep the plant active in regeneration. The more you know about them the better your chances of keeping them well indoors.

It's very easy to find information online by simply typing in the plants name in your favorite search engine!

LEFT PAGE - CLOCKWISE: David's well groomed Bonsai Myrtle topiary • Birdie hunting in the Philadendrons • A beautiful start to a Tilt-a-Whirl Coleus • Brunia albiflora and the succulent Hawarthis attenuata share the stage • THIS PAGE: Detail shot of an Echeveria 'Topsy Turvy'

art by theme

PEOPLE ARE DRAWN TO ART BY DIFFERENT FACTORS. I'M CAPTIVATED BY CERTAIN THEMES, ONE OF WHICH IS NATURE. NOT NEC-ESARILY LANDSCAPE PAINTINGS, BUT BY PEOPLE PAYING HOMAGE IN WHATEVER FORM TO THE PERFECT BEAUTY AROUND US. WHAT I'VE FOUND IS THAT THE VERY IDEA OF COMMON THEMES CAN BE ENOUGH TO SUPPORT THE IDEA OF A "COLLECTION." FOR YEARS WE'VE BEEN BUYING AND OCCASIONALLY TRADING ART BY OUR GOOD FRIENDS WHO ASTOUND US WITH THEIR TALENT. HAVING THE STORY BEHIND THE ARTWORK AND THE ARTIST MAKES IT SO MUCH MORE PERSONAL. WE DON'T BUY ART AS A FINANCIAL INVEST-MENT, INSTEAD WE GO FOR THE INSPIRATIONAL AND CREATIVE INVESTMENT.

ABOVE: A philosophical print by artist Parson Crow • Vintage botanical studies on canvas found at the Brimfield antiques market • One of my flowers in fabric • *Western Sky* oil painting by Ed Shuttleworth • *Wheat* photo by David • *Orchard* by Nora Corbett •
RIGHT: One of my blossom prints from the Nigella fabric line stretched on canvas

tRee House

VIEW

WE HANG HUMMINGBIRD FEEDERS OUT-
SIDE THE LARGE WINDOW. AS A RESULT,
IT'S THE CATS' FAVORITE SPOT TO HANG
OUT DURING THE DAY WHILE WE WORK.
IT'S WHERE I MEDITATE AND STRETCH,
DAVE WRITES, AND WE LISTEN TO
VINTAGE JAZZ ALBUMS EVERY SUNDAY.

ABOVE AND RIGHT: Pete hangs out on a huge bean bag chair I made by picking up an ugly vinyl one and recovering in my Pods fabric. He thinks it's a giant pet bed. I guess it is. • The room is perched above the treeline and affords a stunning view of the valley. Our collections of natural objects lie about, and a Plycraft bentwood leather chair is where I fall asleep watching the geese fly by. • An urchin found on the beach in Cabo. • The cool blues and browns of my Forest fabrics inspired the earthy hues and the Robin's egg wall color. • This Italian wood bowl has a soothing, organic shape that . reminds me of the pods in the bean bag chair.

The furniture is all mid-century redux. We've made two slipcovers for each couch so that we can clean one and still have one out in use. • The floors are also recycled. They're vintage oak planks that came from old factory and barn floors. They were carefully pulled up and barely sanded to keep the vintage patina. • The stainless steel cabinets we had made at a local restaurant supply company. It turned out to be cheaper than we could find in a catalog or shop, and we were able to have them made exactly the right size for the space. We keep books, music, and all of our stereo equipment below. • The top is yet another art gallery for the latest finds, including these beautiful white bird sculptures from the 1960s (RIGHT).

CLOCKWISE LEFT: When you live in a house at the top of a treeline, birds become central to your inspiration. I started picking up these inexpensive ceramics at flea markets and antique shows. They look so vibrant clustered together. • Craspedia Globosa looks like a sculpture in its vase against a Joseph Albers show print. • Medinilla myriantha went crazy in our pots on the front entrance and lasted very well as a cut flower with its dark green foliage bursting off the warm honey coffee table. • Fiona Sunrise Jasmine dances out of its vase. It too, lasts for weeks as a cutting. • THIS PAGE: A wonderful watercolor I picked up by a Japanese street artist reflects the sunny colors of the room.

SLIPCOVERS

{ As a way of life }

Slipcovers are imperative in our home for several reasons.
1. They are the perfect way to change the look quickly.
2. They are a great way to show off new fabrics and seasonal looks.
3. We buy vintage furniture pieces that don't always have the best surfaces, and it's much cheaper than reupholstering.
4. We have three cats. Makes for easy clean up.

It's fun to pick up dramatically shaped chairs to dress them up. You can temper the super mod shapes and vinyl surfaces with the liberal application of prints. Also, with a little skirting around the bottom, you can actually change the aesthetic of the entire chair.

PiLLOWS

{ THE EASIEST WAY TO CHANGE A ROOM }

I'M ALL ABOUT FLEXIBILITY IN DESIGN.
NOTHING IS EASIER THAN USING PILLOWS AS
YOUR QUICK-DRAW DESIGN ELEMENT. I KEEP
THE BACKGROUNDS OF MY SPACES SOME-
WHAT NEUTRAL SO THAT I CAN INJECT THESE
BRIGHT HITS BASED ON ANY WHIM.

I LOVE PILLOWS IN GENERAL, SO WE HAVE
THEM EVERYWHERE — BY DIFFERENT DESIGN-
ERS AND IN DIFFERENT MATERIALS. THE ONES
YOU SEE ON THESE SPREADS ARE ALL IN MY
FABRICS SO THAT YOU CAN SEE HOW FUN AND
BRIGHT THE PILLOW FIGHTS GET IN
OUR HOUSE.

Quilted Throws

{ Graphic, Pretty, Comfy }

I love to design artistic and loose patterns for quilted throws. We don't make any museum art here! Everything is used and loved. Whether they are simple tied throws or heavily quilted designs, I'll be napping away, the cats will be nesting in them and the quilts will add rich detail and artistic spirit to every room. If you would like free patterns for some of the throws you see here, visit my website to download them anytime. www.amybutlerdesign.com

THE BEDROOM

OKAY, MY BEDROOM IS IN TRANSITION. IT WILL LIKELY BE THE LAST ROOM TO BE REFURBISHED.
BUT LIVING IN CHANGE DOESN'T HAVE TO BE UNPLEASANT. I'VE FOUND THAT I LOVE THE BARE WALLS
(MAYBE THAT COMES FROM LOOKING AT LUSCIOUS PATTERNS ALL DAY). WE KEEP OUR ULTIMATE
PASSIVE SPACE AS MINIMAL AND AESTHETICALLY SOOTHING AS WE CAN. EASY TO CLEAN, EASY ON THE EYE.

CLOCKWISE FROM RIGHT: Mod shapes, clean lines, pleasing textures, and simple colors. I had an idea for a flower shape and no paper, so I drew it on the wall. Now David wants me to do the whole wall. We picked up this great mobile at IKEA (as well as the lamps, and the drawers). A vintage chemical beaker holds craspedia globosa. • One of my latest 60s inspired flowers.. • Our collection of small vases make for a pleasing vignette. Succulents hold up well under the soft light and require minimal watering. • The artistic impetus to change our surroundings leads us to simply pin up art on the walls – it's kinetic, easy, and gives even the bedroom an artistic feel. • A french tropical rendering from the early 1930s is among my favorite old prints. • BELOW: It all comes together as organically as it was accumulated. I keep a supply of birch plywood sheets that I use as impromptu frames for pieces of art, so they can move about the house with me.

Hanging out on the bed playing with Birdie in my kashmir print pajamas. I've combined my chrysanthe-mum bolster pillows and square kashmir print pillows with a pillow Dave found in Europe along with bed linens from Urban Outfitters. The large print above the bed is our cat Pete, taken by Dave, and blown up as digital wallpaper (see Resources). • Multiple patterning works! Just keep the color palette simple. Since our walls are soft tones of unfinished plaster, I stuck with deep, yet muted tones that make a splash in the minimal space. Don't obsess over trying to make everything match, just be selective with the color palette to ease the battle over color/pattern/texture. Oh, a little black cat goes with everything.

Who says bed-wear can't be creative? Mix it up–color it up. I have these groovy lounge pants made up.in my Lotus Lace-work print. To illicit romantic dreams, treat yourself to something exotic like these beaded slippers with ruby red bottoms.

Here's another sample of color and pattern as an accent. I used soft goods again to bring in the hit of lush. Minimal design cues lend a confidence and richness of form that really support the splash of prints. • RIGHT: This detail shows one of my fabrics translated to wall art which lends a rich artistic effect. The plaster bird under glass is another example of the running bird themes to my decor and art.

DIGITAL WALLPAPER

{ PERSONALIZED STYLE }

I WANTED TO SEE HOW MY PRINTS WOULD TRANSLATE INTO WALL-
PAPER BUT I HAD NO IDEA HOW TO DO IT. DAVID, BEING A DESIGNER,
HAD A RESOURCE. OUR FRIENDS AT SOLAR IMAGING TOOK A
DIGITAL FILE AND BLEW IT UP IN REPEAT. WORKABLE ON ANY
SUBSTRATE, IT'S A REAL TREAT TO BE ABLE TO PERSONALIZE
A SPACE WITH ANY FORM THAT SUITS YOU. THEY DID THE
IMAGE OF PETE THAT HANGS IN OUR BEDROOM TOO.
BY THE LOOKS OF PETE NAPPING IN THE ROOM,
HE DOESN'T CARE. (SEE RESOURCES FOR INFO)

music motivates!

DAVID AND I ARE BOTH AUDIOPHILES. WE HAVE A VAST COLLECTION OF MUSIC SPANNING THE DECADES: HUGE BINS OF VINTAGE VINYL, CASSETTES, CDS, AND NOW COMPUTERS AND IPODS BURSTING WITH DOWNLOADED TUNES. I LOVE THE IMMEDIACY AND EASE OF MY HIGH-TECH MUSIC GADGETRY, BUT WE'VE DEDICATED A SPACE IN OUR WORLD TO THE CRISP, DEEP SOUNDS OF "OLD-SCHOOL" RECORDS AND BIG SPEAKERS. THEY CAN BE BOUGHT FAIRLY CHEAPLY NOWADAYS, AND IT'S NOT UNTIL YOU HOOK UP AN OLD SYSTEM THAT YOU REMEMBER HOW REALLY AMAZING MUSIC CAN SOUND—AND WITH DAVID'S COLLECTION OF VINTAGE ROCK, HOW LOUD.

ABOVE: I designed my own iPod cover with a cool pocket to hold my mini earphones. • RIGHT: Vintage cool for getting into a 60's vibe. Sorry, AM only.

THE BATHROOM

I THOUGHT THAT REVEALING THE WORLD OF MY BATH MIGHT SEEM A BIT FORWARD. BUT IT IS A PART OF OUR RELAXED LIFE. INSTEAD OF PARADING MY BATHROOM ON THESE PAGES, I'VE CHOSEN TO SHOW A FEW IDEAS THAT I USE TO KEEP MY WORLD ORGANIZED, STYLISH, AND CLEAN. SIMPLE DETAILS, FRESH SCENTS, A TOUCH OF ARTISTIC FLAIR, FLUFFY TOWELS, AND A "DO NOT ENTER" SIGN.

One wall of the bath is another style of non-traditional wallpaper. I found this gorgeous gift wrap at Old Navy during the holiday and thought it was such a luscious print. Instead of wrapping the season in it, I wrapped the bathroom. With some careful cutting and placement, it works just like regular wallpaper, only the small sheets were easier to handle. I did use a strong spray glue instead of the standard wallpaper paste. The accent embroidery is a flea market find.

I love a simple bath with natural details and plants. I keep this large natural sponge next to the bath in a big footed bowl. • The shower curtain is pieced together from two different prints. Simple shower curtains are very easy to make with only a few hems, seams, and grommets. • Laying about the floor, these hand-blown glass balls look like giant bubbles. • Large handled fabric baskets in coordinating prints keep all of our different laundry issues at bay.

The feeling of luxury you get in the bath is not always created by what your bath looks like, but, instead, what you look like!
Make any bathroom feel like a spa with pampering prints and styles like these loungers, simple slippers, and Kimono robe.

FRAGRANCE

{ A WORLD OF COLOR FOR YOUR OLFACTORY SENSES }

CERTAINLY WE ALL HAVE CRAZY DAYS AND DESERVE A LITTLE RESPITE. A GREAT WAY TO STOP THE MADNESS IS TO CLOSE YOUR EYES IN A NICE HOT SOAK OR SHOWER, MEDITATE, OR LISTEN TO MUSIC WITH SOME SOOTHING CANDLES OR AROMATHERAPY OILS. HERE ARE A FEW FAVORITES LISTED WITH THEIR HEALING PROPERTIES, AS WELL AS SOME RECIPES FOR MAKING THE MOST OF SOME TUB R&R. VISIT THIS SITE, WWW.AWORLDOFAROMATHERAPY.COM TO FIND OUT MORE DETAILED INFORMATION.

BERGAMOT
EFFECTS: REFRESHING AND UPLIFTING

CHAMOMILE
EFFECTS: SOOTHING, RELAXING

CLOVE
EFFECTS: WARMING

EUCALYPTUS
EFFECTS: BALANCING, STIMULATING

JASMINE
EFFECTS: SOOTHING, RELAXING

LAVENDER
EFFECTS: CALMING, THERAPEUTIC

LEMONGRASS
EFFECTS: REFRESHING, TONING

PATCHOULI
EFFECTS: RELAXING

PEPPERMINT
EFFECTS: REFRESHING, STIMULATING

SANDALWOOD
EFFECTS: WARMING, RELAXING

YLANG YLANG
EFFECTS: REFRESHING, STIMULATING

FOR A RELAXING BATH:
4 DROPS LAVENDER
3 DROPS BERGAMOT
2 DROPS CEDARWOOD

TO RELIEVE NERVOUSNESS:
6 DROPS GERANIUM
4 DROPS BASIL

FOR INSOMNIA:
8 DROPS CHAMOMILE
4 DROPS LAVENDER
2 DROPS MARJORAM

FOR AN ENERGIZING BATH:
3 DROPS ROSEMARY
2 DROPS LEMON

SOOTHING FOOT BATH:
FILL A CONTAINER (BIG ENOUGH TO HOLD BOTH OF YOUR FEET, OBVIOUSLY) WITH VERY WARM WATER AND ADD A FEW DROPS OF PEPPERMINT OIL.

active spaces

FOOT-TRAFFIC AND PHONE CALLS, LAUGHTER, CHIT-CHAT, MEETINGS, AND EATINGS! THESE ARE THE SPACES THAT SEE THE MOST PEOPLE COME AND GO. THE COLORS ARE LIGHT AND BRIGHT TO KEEP THE SPIRITS HIGH AND TO SHOWCASE ABUNDANT CREATIVITY IN THE BEST POSSIBLE LIGHT.

Activities abound here at the house. Especially because the entire lower level of our home is also the studio and nerve center of our creative business. It's where I design fabrics and patterns and run the business with David and our manager Diane. There is always a flurry of activity, but we try to keep it under control. My work is creative (most of the time), and though I don't let it overwhelm my personal life, it is woven into everything I do. The active spaces, then, are the places that are a-bustle, where I turn on the creative juice and get excited. There are really three active places—the studio, the kitchen, and the garden—but the garden is such a big influence in my work that I've given it its own chapter.

Cooking is creativity for immediate consumption. I love cooking for friends, and we all know how the kitchen becomes the hub of all activity. I wanted to include the kitchen in this book because it is truly the heart of every home, and its primary purpose is not that different from an artist's studio: to provide an inviting place to feed the soul—or, in this case, friends and family. Cooking and gardening are actually very much akin to painting and designing. They are all sparked by curiosity and passion, and I pursue them all with the same excitement and joy.

Active spaces are a joy to design because the impetus is not only to organize but to inspire as well. I hope you'll take away a few ideas in both regards. A clean, simple space that offers the freedom to spread out a bit, and to keep inspiration at hand, is the key to my ideal working environment. As you'll see from the photos, it's not about slick office furniture, high-tech kitchen appliances, or the latest finishes, but about comfort, workability, and style. More than anything, it's about the positive energy from friends and family that you take with you when you follow your artistic dreams.

THE STUDIO

ART OF THE MIDWEST IS THE NAME OF OUR STUDIO.
DAVID AND I STARTED IT IN 1992 WHILE LIVING ON A
FARM IN RURAL OHIO. IT HAS MOVED WITH US FROM
TWO HOUSES AND TWO OTHER STUDIO SPACES. WE
BOUGHT THIS HOUSE BECAUSE WE SAW THE POTENTIAL
TO HAVE OUR CREATIVE SPACE ON THE LOWER WALK-
OUT LEVEL. THE FLOORS ARE PAINTED WHITE TO MAXI-
MIZE THE SUNLIGHT FLOODING INTO THE SOUTH FACING
STAIRWELL. WHEN WE BOUGHT THE HOUSE, IT LOOKED
LIKE A PLACE WHERE THE BRADY BUNCH MIGHT HAVE A
SLEEPOVER OR PRACTICE A SONG AND DANCE ROUTINE.
WE'VE SINCE PUT IN A FEW UPGRADES!

85

amy's studio

My workspace is not particularly big, but it's all mine! It's a clean slate, with touches of primitive warmth and feminine style. It is a studio, so I have my pin-boards and work surfaces, but it's also my nest. Everything I need is at hand, but I hide the technology as best I can, and let the romantic qualities shine through.

ABOVE: Me in my nest. The giant green ottomans are actually made with wooden bases so I can push them together to spread out work or, okay, take a nap with the cats. • RIGHT: I love the feminine touch provided by this handblown glass chandelier. In a simple and modern space, it's really a signature. And, it was a gift from David when we moved in.

ABOVE: Bits of inspiration and ephemera from my shelves and desk. I love the detail and patterns in vintage pins, tin boxes, and notebooks. I also have a stationery fetish and so I was very excited when I got the opportunity to do my own line! • RIGHT: My space in a flood of light. The vintage farm table is large enough to hold my work and computer. David put clips underneath it to hide all the wires. Vintage wood cabinets hold my inspirations while stainless restaurant shelving holds my books and purses on the walls. I've tempered the country feeling with modern patterns, chairs, and finishes.

CLOCKWISE: The brown cabinet holds my work files and computer printer next to a dress form and newest dress design. • The pinboard wall is where I hang all of my work and latest inspired finds. We wrapped homosote board with canvas and screwed them into the walls. Below that we mounted some IKEA kitchen cabinets so I'd have a space to store patterns and set fabrics on top. • A collection of my grandmother's embroideries are hanging up beside a mod vintage Vera scarf and some of my favorite antique kimono and Obi textiles from Japan. • I keep rolls of my own fabric handy on a large restaurant supply cart so I can "serve them up" as the need arises!

ABOVE: I have several "collector's corners" where I keep my finds. When I create new fabric items like handbags and pillows, I love to combine vintage ribbons and pins with new fabrics. But I have so many that unless they're in plain sight, I'll forget that I have them. This vintage mail sorter houses not only ribbons, but yarns, fabric scraps, and trinkets collected on my journeys. The only problem with this design is that the cats treat it like a grocery shelf of wonderful toys to be pulled from and strewn about the house. • RIGHT: In the glass flatback cabinet behind my desk is a showcase of vintage costume jewelry and decorative prizes including beautiful pincushions that I've received as gifts. I love to make lush color stories in the cabinet and pull from them for accents to my handbags.

central Hub

THIS IS WHERE WE HAVE OUR MEETINGS AND LAY PROJECTS OUT ON THE TABLE.
DIANE RUNS THE BUSINESS RIGHT IN FRONT OF EVERYONE, AND WE HAVE
AN OPEN-DOOR POLICY THAT BRINGS A CONSTANT EBB AND FLOW OF LOCAL
WOMEN WHO SEW FOR US. THE ART IS EVER-CHANGING, THE SURFACES WORN,
THE LIGHT SOFT, AND THE SPIRITS HIGH.

LEFT: The most kinetic space we have! With all of the fabrics and patterns coming
and going, this space changes almost daily. It's amazing that we could stop long
enough to take these photos. • ABOVE: A few of my vintage paintings laying in wait
on display. I love the little shell trees and our folk art portraits.

95

We work in these spaces everyday, and it's our home. We want to make people feel welcome and cared for when they are here. Whenever possible we try to have cut flowers on hand. They have a calming effect, especially fragrant roses. • RIGHT: Certain visual cues create the feeling of a modern farm setting. The use of large primitive furnishings and the natural storework combine with modern touches and attitude. The central worktable is where we have our meetings, edit sewing patterns, exchange ideas, and plan our schedules. It opens to the stairwell which provides great light for working on new designs. My collection of vintage McCoy and other mid-century pottery makes a nice color story on the industrial shoe factory rack.

CLOCKWISE: Here's an idea we came up with in the hub: things come and go, get stuffed into bags, and take some abuse. And as we all know—have laptop will travel! I was beating it up so much, that we decided to give it a very origami-style wrapper. With just a few seams and a little velcro you can make a customized wrap to travel in style. This one has a thin layer of batting for cushion. • RIGHT: This early 60s papier mâché figure has become the very essence of what I consider Midwest Modern. It was a very thoughtful gift from my father, and she feels very warm, friendly, cool, graceful, and confident. All the traits we aspire to in our lives.

11 12
10
9
8

Design Lab

David's side of the studio is where all of the marketing, design, patterns, Web sites, and photography are produced. It's where the "boys" hang out, and we can pull the giant doors shut to keep them out of the "girls' club" (until we need something). Along with all of the design and production for my lines, David also creates design work nationally for retail, editorial, and advertising clientele.

CLOCKWISE: A few things we've learned over the years: you need to have the right furniture for the job, and wheels are good! David's love of music and surfing give a splash of color to a corner reserved for heavy cutting and assembly. We keep recycling bins at easy access below the high-profile hospital table which is perfect for bringing detailed work up so we don't have to stoop. A simple piece of foamcore pinned behind the wall holds reference material and tools.

The design lab houses David's workspace and desk which is made from an old medical guerney. We made birch plywood backwalls that rest on inexpensive tool cabinets to use as pinboards and warm up the white space. It's a great surface for David to review photography or layouts. • We found these vintage elevator safety doors at a junk shop in Cleveland and turned them into one enormous room divider by fastening them together with angle-iron and hanging them from a barn door slider. • My original vintage 70s sewing machine, purchased at a garage sale still gets pulled out for active duty.

A sneak peak into the process. ABOVE: This painting awaits translation into a repeat pattern. I could pull out elements from it to make accent prints as well. The colors will change dramatically by the time it's turned into fabric. I love having them around the house to study and get ideas. They make great art. • RIGHT: One of my patterns that needed to be translated into line art on the computer in the design lab. • My color chips and color sketches alongside the final fabric art. • I rely on David and our designer Jake to help with these computer-generated technical renderings as I still do everything by hand.

Patterns as paper. From wrapping gifts to stationery, scrapbooks to notebooks. I love the application of vibrant prints to the everyday things. There are so many levels of scale to the use of pattern. I started out by painting surface patterns that were sold to many different types of companies for use on wallpaper, dishes, paper goods, clothing, bedding, and so on. Now it's coming full circle and I'm getting to do it all over again. Except this time, my name is on it! I love making collections,and thinking about design as not simply one print, but as many pieces that work in unison.

kitchen

THE HEART OF THE HOME. LIKE THE STUDIO,
I LOVE HAVING EVERYTHING AT HAND.
COOKING IS VERY MUCH AN ART FORM, BUT
THE PALETTES DELIGHT *ALL* OF THE SENSES.
THIS GREAT SPACE FLOODED WITH NATURAL
LIGHT REMINDS ME OF OLD FARMHOUSES WITH
SUMMER KITCHENS. I REMEMBER AS A LITTLE
GIRL THE INCREDIBLE AROMAS
COMING FROM THE OPEN KITCHEN WINDOWS
AND DRIFTING OUTSIDE TO WHERE I WAS
PLAYING. MY MOTHER, AN AMAZING COOK,
(SHE WOULD NEVER CALL HERSELF A CHEF)
INSPIRED ME TO FIND THE SAME LOVE IN
COOKING THAT I PURSUED IN THE VISUAL ARTS.
KITCHENS DON'T HAVE TO BE DESIGNER-
LABELED OR GADGET-LADEN, BUT THE FRESH
CHARACTER OF A CLEAN, OPEN SPACE INSPIRES
AN UNABASHED PASSION TO SHARE A MEAL.

CLOCKWISE: Ready at the helm. The beauty of open shelving is akin to having your brushes and paints by your side. It also keeps you from cluttering up your space with vessels and objects you don't really need. I'd rather have only a few really high-quality cooking utensils than a load of cheap ones (mostly because I know I'd dirty them all up). • Vintage tablecloths add a shot of passion and warmth to any setting—and I love to collect them. • Keep accents to a minimum so the food takes center stage, use surfaces that are easy to clean, and play music while you cook!

You can see how a simplicity of backdrop and colors allows for the romance of food and cooking to shine through. The spartan space lets a few simple details stand out, like the 60s enamel bowl on the 50s fridge, or the weave in the market tote.

CLOCKWISE: Color as accent! Small details really shine when they're given the chance. Cool blues and a smattering of lime green add depth to the whites and browns of the kitchen. • Dark chocolate and caramel-infused soft cheese (you heard right) with a little honey looks as good as it tastes!

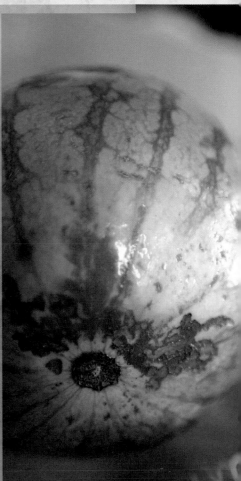

Simple foods, bright colors. Key to our eating habits are buying and preparing locally grown or raised organic foods whenever possible. Support of local farming and organic practices simply makes sense to you and your immediate surroundings. We visit our farm market each weekend when it's in season, and try to buy only what we need for that week. It has become part of the ritual of our week and turns into our social time to visit with neighbors and friends. It's hard sometimes to slow down and see the benefits of eating well, but buying the food you eat from the person that grew it, meeting them and hearing about their season, the soil, the harvest, keeps you rooted in the connection between you and the things you take in.

(See the resource guide on page 222 for more info and Web sites about organic and local farming.)

aprons

Aprons are so much more than splash guards. In my opinion they are to daily fashion what pillows are to interiors. An instant upgrade. Not to mention the feeling you have when you put one on. It's the female version of the men's leather work glove.

These are a few of the aprons that we've made here in the studio from my fabrics, as well as some vintage redux versions (seen on Taylor and Nora - insert above).

BODY as canvas

I WENT TO ART SCHOOL FOR FASHION. I ENJOY FASHION BECAUSE
OF ITS ABILITY TO TRANSFORM US. YOUR SPIRIT CAN RISE AND YOUR
CONFIDENCE GROW WHEN YOU ARE WEARING SOMETHING YOU LOVE.
EACH PERSON CAN HAVE A UNIQUE SENSE OF STYLE. I DON'T FIND
IT MY PLACE TO JUDGE PERSONAL FASHION, OR COMPARE WHAT
SOMEONE IS WEARING TO THE GREATER FASHION CULTURE. I LOVE
TO SEE INDIVIDUALS EMPOWER THEMSELVES BY EXPRESSING THEIR
OWN ARTISTIC VOICE.

Clothing, even in the most utilitarian way, is how we show ourselves to the rest of the world. Sometimes the message is "I don't have time to think about what I'm wearing" or "I don't care right now, thank you very much." Like when you wear your sweats to the grocery. We've all been there. But this is about inspiration! Not in a haute couture way, but with a Midwest Modern attitude. Style is about combining ideas and whims, desires and passions into something that represents you. It's not about how much it cost, who made it, or where you bought it—we all know how easy it is to succumb to the marketing zeitgeist. This book is about finding your own voice, on your own terms. I simply want to give you a few ideas and show you some examples of combining old with new to create unique looks. Oh yes, all of the models are friends and girls from the area who wear and love these styles.

Many of the designs in this section are made from my sewing patterns. I started creating sewing patterns as a way to inspire other people to use and recycle material scraps. That led into designing handbag patterns, which led into home decor items, which led into clothing! Once I started designing fabrics, well, of course I had to use them to make my projects. What I found is not every woman who got on my website and saw the handbag patterns felt they could make them. So I decided to manu-facture limited runs of finished items and sell them on my site as well. I've included some samples in this section (along with a little bit of history).

So the reality of "Mid Mod" fashion is this: we shop in various places, combine looks, love vintage, and devise our own sense of style based on moods and desires. We create the looks we can't find, and take great joy in the homemade. It's fun to pay attention to fashion culture, but sheeplike to follow it too closely. Nobody looks much at the Midwest for fashion trend, and that's okay. We Midwesterners are plenty busy looking at ourselves.

Long
Tall
duster

Chelsea

Vintage

pleats

Everything begins with a sketch. My sketches are loose and give a general idea of the basic look I'm going for. I then work with my amazing seamstresses to figure out the best ways to make the garments or bags. We tweak actual fabric models of the designs. Sometimes a design looks great in your head, and even on paper, but it's tricky to make it real. Capturing organic shaped bags still requires a bit of math, and lots of patience.

125

vintage Redux

I've always been a fan of repurposed and vintage clothing. It's smart, unique, and inexpensive, and the likelihood that you'll see someone else in the same outfit is zero! Combined with something new, or something in the back of your closet, it breathes new life into your wardrobe. Sometimes you love the print, but not the style. What to do? Change the style. Usually with nothing more than minor tweaks, you can create a distinctive and modern cut on a vintage piece. On the following pages are some cool examples.

126

before

after

Lime floral for Emily

Vintage Redu

EMILY'S SUMMER SKIRT

We found this great green floral for Emily but the dress cut and overall style was a bit too "Mrs. Brady" for her. So, we turned it into a fab skirt. This one dresses up and down very easily. I decided to remove the belt to keep it from looking like an apron, but it could be a nice touch tied in the back. For about $15 she had an amazing one-of-a-kind summer skirt!

Low hem on the deep green

TAYLOR'S LAYERING SKIRT

This vintage dress had a great natural hemline. Taylor decided it would be a great complement to these vintage pajama bottoms. The complementary colors are bright and the striking graphics on the orange/red pants are a cool surprise under the subtle hues of green in the skirt. A simple top keeps it from going over the top. When Taylor does wear shoes (not often), subtle flats or natural sandals work best. *Almost* as cute as she is.

before

DRENDA'S VINTAGE HOUSEDRESS

With only a few minor tweaks, we were able to create this vintage modern dress that suited Drenda to a T. The heavy-weight fabric hangs well, but makes taking in the waist a bit more difficult. The gorgeous print is well-suited to the scale of this dress. The length falls at her mid-calf which accentuates her tall, slender build. A sleeveless cut also supports the tall, thin feel, and keeps it from feeling matronly.

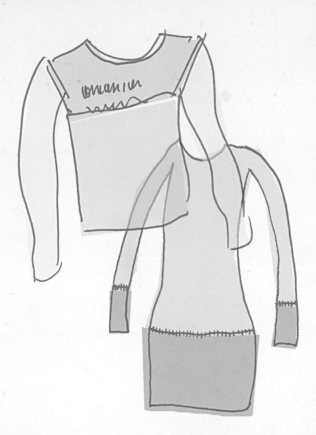

puzzle tees

WHO DOESN'T LOVE A GOOD T-SHIRT? I SPEND
MOST OF MY TIME IN THEM. SOFT COTTON TEES ARE
COMFY WORKHORSES TO ANY ACTIVE LIFESTYLE. SO
TO BRING A LITTLE UNIQUE FASHION INTO YOUR
DAILY GRIND, TRY SOME SIMPLE TEE REDUX. HERE
WE'VE CUT UP A FEW OLD STYLES AND GIVEN THEM
NEW LIFE WITH CHANGED SHAPES AND A SIMPLE
CONTRASTING TOP-STITCH.

FAR LEFT: Bethany wears a fitted 3/4 sleeve style made
from three different T-shirts. We cut the collar and let it
roll for a beach-inspired french neck. • NEAR LEFT: Taylor is wearing a fitted dress made with two tees.
The sleeves made extra-long to fall over her hands with
button-holes cut for her thumbs gives it a modern flair.
The skirt portion is nothing more than the body of the
same tee that provided the extra sleeve length. This
design is great for bedtime too.

scratch style

MADE-FROM-SCRATCH DESIGNS. AND IN MY CASE CHICKEN SCRATCH IS APPROPRIATE—I SKETCH DESIGNS QUICKLY, AND I CATCH MY STUDIO MATES SQUINTING TO DECIPHER MY CRYPTIC SCRIBBLE NOTES AND DRAWINGS. THESE MADE-FROM-SCRATCH ORIGINALS ARE FINISHED PROJECTS USING MY FABRICS THAT WE CREATED EITHER AS TESTS FOR SEWING PATTERNS OR AS ONE-OFFS TO HIGHLIGHT THE PRINTS. IT GIVES US A GREAT EXCUSE TO STRETCH OUR FASHIONISTA WINGS. I'VE COMBINED THEM WITH OVER-THE-COUNTER PIECES TO HIGHLIGHT THE FACT THAT GREAT STYLE CAN COME FROM MANY SOURCES. EDITING IS KEY, AND IT'S THAT ONE SIGNATURE PIECE THAT CAN SET YOUR TONE.

ABEJE'S WRAP

This simple piece was created with motion and spirit in
mind. I wanted a light accent piece with a clean and
modern cut that would allow for graceful movement. Our
sophisticated dancer Abeje looks and moves amazing in
this one made up in my Grand Tapestry fabric.

CABO HALTER
This is one of my sewing patterns. Abeje wears it so well with her jewelry and bright smile. Simple lines and a slightly flared waist make for a great warm weather day-into-night piece.

LIVERPOOL DRESS

David named this dress after deciding that it looked like something the Beatles' girlfriends might wear in the early 60s. I wanted a modern take on the classic lines of the 50s style house dress. This one we made up in my Sunbloom fabrics. Here you see me cleaning up with David's guitar. I added some simple mother-of-pearl buttons to give it an elegant detail.

MID MOD DRESS

If there is one particular dress that sums up my
Midwest Modern voice it might be this one. I love
the simple lines and cap sleeves. Like so many of
my other designs, it works perfectly with jeans.
This image pairs it with some groovy slipcovered
lampshades and a circular stool for that
complete nature-inspired, mod feel.

SKIRTOLOGY

You can never have too many skirts, can you? These are a few of my designs including the Barcelona (center) which plays with the unfinished seams as a finishing detail.

BOLD IS PRETTY

Don't be afraid of color! It is your friend. Like so many other adventures in design, the key is in the editing. Start with basic complementing palettes and pair solids with pattern. Layering is fine, but usually it's best to keep it within one area like a layered skirt with a simple top. Fresh flowers are always acceptable.

PATCHWORK DUSTER

I love the idea of taking something that might be thought of as conservative or masculine and turning it into something flashy and feminine. This patchwork duster with a very exagerated collar has rock-star presence but maintains a clean line with its cut. The color and pattern is so off-the-chart but the entire look is confident and playful.

SUNDAY DRESS

These pages illustrate how the same dress cut takes on a different look with different fabrics. I love the inverted neckline that narrows as it gets closer to the shoulders, and the subtle curve at the top of the chest. It speaks to a much more glamorous evening wear cut, but with humble, mod prints in simple cotton. Just a little wink.

THE BLUE SKY HAT

I made one of these sun hats because
I wanted a hat of my own design made
up in my fabrics for a vacation trip.
So many people liked it that I had to
create a pattern! That has turned into
the way I develop my sewing pattern
ideas—I make up samples and post
them on my website to see which ones
ilicit a huge response. It's always
obvious which ones evoke passion.
• RIGHT: Here are some variations of
the same design in different fabrics.

CAPS

Underestimated as a fashion piece, the skull cap is versatile and easy. It's the perfect cure for post work-out or early morning hair. You don't have to be a bike messenger to look cool in one either! • ABOVE: Serene wears a knit beanie with a fabric flower (from my Madison Bags pattern). • RIGHT: Bethany wears a skull cap (from my Blue Sky Hats pattern) in a vintage fabric, along with stunning ponytails and a paisley Cabo Halter top.

SCARVES

Another under-used staple from the past is the scarf. In all its variety, I consider it the perfect accessory to glam up and add a layer of elegance to everyday wear. You look just a little bit smarter, and stay just a little bit warmer. • LEFT: Emily wears a patchwork design in soft blue cottons. • RIGHT: Sharon wears a more winter-friendly flannel in lime green.

AROUND THE NECK

BELOW: This simple project is done by simply knotting a tube of patchworked fabrics, sliding in a styrofoam ball, and continuing until you've reached the desired length. You could use marbles to achieve a heavier hanging style. I've sewn multiple fabrics into one tube, but you could also simply make different fabric necklaces and wear them all at once. • RIGHT: My friend and jewelry designer Kim Mettee made this glorious piece for me. It's a great example of unique colors and textures coming together in a completely new way to give something a vintage feel. Handmade jewelry is one of my all-time great passions and with the investment of a few simple tools, patience, (and maybe a few classes), it becomes a great way to gift friends and family with one-of-a-kind artifacts of love.

CHOOSING JEWELRY

Accentuating your style and look with jewelry is very personal. The look should reflect and harmonize your form. My idea of beautiful jewelry is the opposite of glitz and bling. It doesn't have to be expensive, but appropriate. • LEFT: Notice how Taylor's simple pearl drops mirror her delicate round eyes. Her skintone is fair, and the light, loose attitude of the simple strand feels right with her peasant ease. • RIGHT: Abeje wears a satin finish pair of oblong loops that work with the curves of her face structure. They feel regal, but casual at the same time.

COLOR AND TEXTURE

Great style can come from confidence. Use bright accents to draw attention, but not too much. • ABOVE AND RIGHT: The blue on blue feels cool and collected, while the bold blue necklace on Abeje feels more dramatic and sunny against the bright green pillow.

in the bag

MANY OF YOU MIGHT KNOW ME FOR MY BAG DESIGNS. THIS BOOK GIVES
ME A WONDERFUL OPPORTUNITY TO SHOWCASE SOME OF THE PATTERNS
THAT I HAVE CREATED OVER THE YEARS AND THAT SO MANY OF YOU HAVE
TURNED INTO YOUR OWN FRESH STYLE. I WOULD LOVE FOR YOU TO FIND
THE INSPIRATION TO CREATE YOUR OWN. I COULD TELL YOU THAT MY
SEWING PATTERNS ARE A GREAT PLACE TO START, BUT THAT WOULD BE
PANDERING, NOW WOULDN'T IT? (SEE RESOURCES)

BIG BAGS

The foundation for any good bag is good function.
But then it has to be made well, and look stunning.
It's tricky getting all of those elements to align, and
the most effective way to learn what that mix is,
well, is to carry and use the heck out of a design
before unleashing it onto the world. We're in constant bag development here at the studio—and we
couldn't be happier to dive into our "research."

MESSENGER BAGS

I love making practical and highly functional bags that look good. This messenger has simple pleats on the bottom edge that give it a military, finished look. It was designed with the student in mind, but a lot of women (and men) use them as briefcases.

THE ULTIMATE ACCESSORY

In the long chain of human history, bags are almost as old as clothing. Historically they've been used for a vast multitude of purposes from carrying water, tools, food, coin, weapons, to of course lipstick. A purse can say many things about the carrier—trendy, independent, stylish, extroverted, fun, serious, or even wild. I want my bags to be joyful, stylish, and confident. I want the same for every woman who makes or carries one. Make your own purse, and you define your look!

FABRICS

FABRIC DESIGN IS WOVEN INTO EVERYTHING I DO, AND IT NEVER TIRES. I LOVE CREATING COLLECTIONS AND CHANGING UP MY STYLE EACH TIME I SIT DOWN TO DEVISE A PRINT. THESE PRINTS ARE A CULMINATION OF ORIGINAL DRAWINGS, RECONFIGURED VINTAGE DESIGNS, AND UNIQUE COLOR COMBINATIONS THAT I WEAVE INTO A STORY. I LIKEN EACH PRINT TO A PAGE IN A PICTURE BOOK, AND A COLLECTION TO THE COMPLETE STORY. WHEN THE PRINTS COME BACK FROM THE FACTORY AS SAMPLE STRIKE-OFFS, I'M A LITTLE GIRL IN MY OWN CANDY STORE. THE MOST EXCITING THING IS THAT OTHER ARTISTS, CRAFTERS, QUILTERS, DESIGNERS, AND LOVED ONES FIND INSPIRATION IN THEM AS WELL. WHAT AN HONOR.

HARMONY

Different time periods inspired different ideas about what people desired. Fashions changed, colors changed. I am inspired by *all* the eras of the 19th and 20th century, not just a few. The trick to working all of these design styles into a cohesive collection is harmonizing scale, color, shape, and pattern. Now, is there a magic bullet theory or textbook that can teach it? Not really. It's a feeling. I rely on design intuition from years of doing it, and years of art school preparing me to do it. A few large scale anchor prints, a mini-print, good symmetrical pieces, and some more organic repeats can all work together to tell a new story. I make plenty of mistakes, scratch my head, and edit like crazy to get to the final collection. I love the process, and the product!

MAKE IT

Cotton fabrics were used and worn by Egyptians earlier than 2,500 BC. They didn't have sewing machines. Realize that the sewing arts are not profoundly difficult, and once you master a few simple stitches by hand, and get the feel for using a machine, a great foundation has been laid. When you start out you will make mistakes, I still do. But there's hardly anything more satisfying than having made something that you wear or carry. It's empowering to create your own fashion and follow through on your own ideas. Even if you stumble at first, stick with it, you'll only get better.

natural HiGHLiGHtS

Gardening is seasonal, just like fabrics. And like design, gardening relies on learning, study, and creativity. (Of course, the challenges of Midwestern climate don't exist in the safety of my studio—the worst that might happen there is that I spill some tea on a print or one of the cats chews on a corner.) Gardening creates kinetic art through combinations of elements. I certainly do not create the design. It's really about the collection, and how it all works together: scale, color, texture, time, and all the other dynamics that make a garden grow.

Several of my close friends have the same passion for gardening. So, as in every other creative aspect of my life, we share ideas and materials. Plant swaps are common, as are seasonal runs to particular greenhouses in surrounding areas and neighboring states. Frankly, in springtime it's a little hard for me to focus on designing indoors when I'm daydreaming of amended soil, hellebores, banana trees, boxwood, and hydrangeas. Some of the garden shots here are from my friends' homes as well. It's where I draw endless inspiration for my design (as you'll see).

In the same spirit of originality that inspires me to create bright, worldly prints here in my humble Ohio studio, I combine unusual, worldly specimens in my Midwestern garden. David and I enjoy creating a tropical mood that suits the style of our house. It feels surprising yet familiar here in the hills of Ohio, and it inspires me to keep thinking outside my comfort zone—or at least our climate zone. Passersby appreciate the fact that the garden stands out, but still blends with the native plants such as buckeye trees, forsythia, and native grasses that we plant alongside. It's all about harmony of colors, textures, and shapes. That's why this section will highlight garden design as inspiration for my fabrics. The thinking is the very same!

mount parnassus

The urban gardens that envelop our modern home are lush and laden, combining tropical and regional specimens. Groves of bananas dance with dahlias and hydrangea. Japanese maples and specimen pines complement stone walls hand-built by David to retain cyprus, daphne, poppies, and anemone on our steep hillsides. And yes, I spend as much time trimming and weeding as it appears!

The view from the north-facing deck in an early morning fog fills the bottom of this page. As well, the view looking out of our front door into the front gardens highlights the "lush factor." My Lotus print was inspired by the calming effects of the garden in summer. • RIGHT: Buddah sits by the front door greeting all who enter. • Honré Jobért Anemones leap out of the thick green beds. • Lady's Mantle, Sweet Woodruff, and Carex surround one of our mossy stones. • We've been told our home feels like India in Ireland.

CLOCKWISE FROM LEFT: Musa Basjoo banana trees are perennial in our zone 5 climate! We cut them back every November and they come back 10-15 feet tall (no bananas). Our beds are filled with various elephant ears, Euphorbias, Peonies, and grasses. • Large, dark-stemmed Colocasia Esculenta and Cypress Alternifolia reach from their urns at the front door. • A single heirloom Poppy caught our attention with its graceful curved stem. • Purple allium reach above my very young tree Peony (for now).

CLOCKWISE FROM LEFT: This study in white on green begins with the humble Hosta bloom. • Next to that, the mother Hosta springs up to keep an eye out for our ever-present deer. • A large Dahlia blossom takes center stage as usual. • Alliums (chives) blowing in the breeze. • Wonderfully fragrant Nicotiana (flowering tobacco) is a long-lasting and rewarding white beauty. • A stand of Epimedium hides below bright white Azalea blossoms. • My Tree Peony fabric pays homage to one of my perenial favorites. It's draped behind a cluster from my Nigella line. • An itzy-bitzy spider makes its way across the ribbon grass.

TROPIC OF OHIO

There's a very definite tropical feeling that we work a bit harder to maintain here in Ohio. It just means looking a little further for great plants and taking good care of potted varieties, digging and moving things in for the winter, and letting our storage room become "grow light central." The ooohhs and aaahhs are worth it.

CLOCKWISE FROM LEFT: Gold Hakonechloa and its sharp chartruese colored leaves • LIme and yellow Euphorbia inspired my logo color • A large red-stocked Ensete feels like a planting at a royal Indian palace • A collection of my tropical inspired fabrics prints • Musa Basjoo (this page) Banana leaves filter the sunlight • A small Crassula Jade • Colocasia Illustris and its amazing deep colors are very exotic •Another stand of Euphorbia • CENTER: A hearty Canna which has a beautiful habit of beading up water like small pools of mercury in its curled leaves

BOXWOOD. cottage

My good friends Kevin Reiner and Chuck Ross own this amazing home in our village, where they have transformed a blank canvas into these Cotswold-inspired gardens. Kevin is a garden designer and horticulturist (can you tell?). His gardens are indicative of his graceful style and sensitivity. The layout is intimate and grand at the same time.

CLOCKWISE FROM UPPER LEFT: Forget-me-nots in hand-laid stone paths • The gardens in the back of the house • Arching Beauty Bush frames a Sweet Bay Topiary • A "Charm" coneflower fabric • The silvery finish of an old teak bench • The wild, woody backdrop of the Boxwood property

CLOCKWISE FROM LEFT: One of Kevin's amazing Tree Aloe plants nestled in an avalanche of Sedum • The graphic ribbing of Honey Bush casts a great shadow • Baby Tears overflow at the front steps • My French Wallpaper print, which feels like a paisley version of a succulent plant • Heavy stacked stone walls are the foundation of Kevin's garden architecture • Establishing planter combinations (like the Tree Aloe and Sedum) that are both striking and have the same watering, feeding, soil, and sunlight needs might seem intimidating—so check out www.firmlyplanted.net for great combinations that will work together.

HOPEWELL SPRINGS

A sprawling countryside estate is the setting for these large garden vignettes. My friends Michael Rosen and Mark Svede have created nothing short of a well-appointed city park, complete with a large pond and organic sculptures. There are acres and acres of unique settings that meander around sunlit lanes and open to well-kept beds of annuals and perenials.

CLOCKWISE FROM LEFT: The summer dining shed stands ready to entertain among the lively Miscanthus, Geraniums, Sedum, and Caryopteris • The shared strength of Wisteria vines • Mark's eternally unlit bonfire stacks make for amazing displays of organic architecture throughout the property • Wild cat looking befuddled • Wonderful texture and patina of the old shed roof • A Night-blooming Cereus in all of its glory—caught here in a one-night-only show • Deep blue adirondack sets wait by the water's edge • I named this fabric Royal Garden, its inspiration stemming from the gorgeous old gardens of England, and dreams of visiting my friends at Hopewell, right here in Ohio.

Even though the critters take their toll, there's something captivating about the their feasting on such vivid Dahlias. These pages capture the vivid pinks, reds, and purples of the mid-summer garden. CLOCKWISE FROM UPPER LEFT: Soil acidity aides in determining the coloration of Hydrangea blossoms • A palette of my brightest fabrics inspired by the hot hues of summer • BIG SHOTS: Dahlias and the company they keep! • Asiatic Lillies in soft pink • One of my enormous Tree Peony blossoms • Hearty Begonias reaching out • LOWER RIGHT: Obediant Plant in deep magenta • Little blue/purple puffs of Ageratum

More beauties! Just a sketchbook sampler of Dahlias, Zinnias, and Ranunculus in comparison to one of my exploding prints. Not only are plants an ever-changing palette of inspiration, but so too are the places in which you find them. Different gardeners are akin to different artists. They translate their palettes to reflect certain ideas of beauty. Some are very flashy and others are very subdued. It's all in the eye of the beholder. But it's hard to deny a bright, fresh blossom!

GYPSY caravan

To find inspiration, sometimes you have to go out and look for it. Clear your mind, take in new experiences. Being an artist isn't about obsessing, it's about *revealing*, about exposing your soul to the universe. It can make you feel vulnerable sometimes. The best way to feel at peace with your creativity is to embrace your place in the world. Experience the beauty of your surroundings, tune in to other people, and fully immerse yourself in the world to which you offer your art. That way, you'll never feel as though your art doesn't fit in.

"Gypsy Caravan" refers to a mindset. Drop everything and go. You may not even know where you're going, but grab some supplies and head out the door. Take friends with you. It doesn't need to be glamorous, or expensive. Matter of fact, the best getaways are usually on the fly. Take off on Friday and go antiquing with friends until Sunday night. Hit the greenhouses on the way. Eat at diners and picnic at rest stops. Camp if you like to rough it.

Don't get me wrong, I love a nice hotel, an exotic vacation, an amazing meal (who doesn't like all that?). But there are so many great places just a stone's throw from where you are. It's more about the impetus of just getting out the door. I like to have a very loose idea about where I'm headed, and a few destinations, but no schedule. When you work for yourself you soon realize that schedules become a way of life, and everyone wants to break free of them somehow. The great irony is that we all think work should be organized, but it is usually chaos—whereas we want our free time to be chaos, but somehow it's always more organized! It's because we're so focused on being free, and excited to put energy into it.

This is one such trip: a jaunt with David in our vintage camper en route to a flea market, culminating in a weekend sleepover with friends at the lake. Three great phases, each of which did its part to feed my soul. The adventure of camping and the silence to clear my mind. Then the joy of meeting people and finding new inspirations at the flea market. Followed by the familiar comfort of friends—wiling away the hours laughing and reminiscing. All of these things ground me, calm my heart, and help me realize that the great gift in my life isn't art or style, but people. And that takes away any pressure to "make art." Which is the great secret to fresh ideas and creative fire.

camp butler

David and I are big on the outdoors, but his camping style is fairly primitive. I got the idea to create a modern take on Victorian camping by sprucing up his vintage Land Cruiser with some soft edges, and creating a few simple details to make our trip a bit more "civilized." It's a fun way to make something you are used to doing a bit more creative and fresh. I didn't want to go over the top, and we did have to leave room for flea market finds, but our little gypsy camp took on the feeling of a romantic expedition.

BELOW: Setting up camp with a canvas tent I designed to attach to our '77 Toyota. Easy folding butterfly chairs and a few throw pillows add some comfort. • RIGHT: Straw hats, soda pop, and a good book. What else do you need? Maybe a good, tall pair of rubber boots.

Civilization is not overrated! Ever since I saw *Out of Africa* I've wanted to make our outdoor or adventure travels just a bit more stylish. You can't blame a girl. So I created these simple curtains on a spring extension rod for a bit of privacy in the back of David's truck. • Enamel tin cups, melamine and aluminum plates and our old cutlery are kept tidy in an old wire basket. • We light up the evenings with collapsible lanterns.

flea market

ALWAYS ON THE HUNT FOR GREAT INSPIRATIONS FOR OUR HOME AND STUDIO, WE ROLLED INTO THE HILLS OF CENTRAL OHIO LOOKING FOR A FEW OF OUR FAVORITE, ANTIQUE FLEA MARKETS. YOU SIMPLY CAN'T BEAT THE MIDWEST FOR ANTIQUE SHOWS AND SHOPS. AVID FLEA SHOPPERS THAT WE ARE, DAVID AND I HAVE YEARS OF EXPERIENCE TO DRAW UPON—OR COMPLETELY IGNORE—WHEN DISCOVERING THAT PERFECT NUGGET OF COOL. THE SIGHTS, SOUNDS, AND SMELLS OF A GREAT OUTDOOR SHOW IN THE LATE SUMMER ARE AMONG MY FAVORITE ENTICEMENTS.

RIGHT, CLOCKWISE FROM TOP: Vintage juice glasses with bright flowers catch my eye • My giant Betty Shopper bag is the ultimate flea market tote • A great impromptu display for a fedora • We bought this groovy 1960s fiberglass planter • Mid-century dishware in gorgeous colors • Costume jewelry is my weakness! I bought this pin to put on one of my bags • Fresh peaches • Super groovy fabric on these seat cushions • An Indian etched wood piece • I love the 1970s colors on this Kava coffee mug • A cool wooden piece for our miniature vase collection • A sullen cherub awaits purchase, and a new home

FLEA MKT.

CLOCKWISE: I love the bird inlays on the pick-guards of this old acoustic guitar (no strings attached) • A great combo of prints in this 1970s cloth • A lively, pink Dahlia pin that I had to wear right away • Graceful and mod looking wind chimes • A crazy green owl vase harkens back to my childhood drawings • A board of stunning glass beads catches the warm afternoon sun

Lake House Retreat

We ended the long weekend with a sleepover at our friends' lake house. Drinking wine on the dock while soaking our feet, making fabulous meals, boating, and reading. No elaborate parties, no dramatic decorations or themes. We simplify, and spend our time getting to know each other all over again. Nothing glamorous. But then, what could be better?

My good friend Amy and I take a nature walk to the shore • Boats in the harbor, and boat ashore • Dutch influences and dramatic colors on the way to the lake • Cows on vacation, I can only assume

When it's all said and done, my dream is to be surrounded by my friends and family. We live as artists and make our dreams the best way we know how. Time always gets away from you, because tomorrow never comes, and yesterday is gone. All we have is right now. So for us, a simple retreat to share stories and simply be there for each other is the perfect answer. Time spent reflecting, dreaming up new ideas, new designs, new gardens, and new memories.

epilogue

Defining Midwest Modern as a style might seem a bit difficult at first. Honest, approachable, creative, but not confined by parameters set by the culture at large. To define it as a lifestyle might be easier. Being an artist in the Midwest is not very different from being one in southern Europe. Think of a painter on the Rhine, or a sculptor outside of Avignon. Drawing inspiration from your surroundings, but not conforming to the collective rules of a society. Creating in order to express beauty and finding peace in the sheer joy of it. Looking at things differently, and not having to look hard.

First and foremost, I wanted this book to inspire you—not to look at my life and work in awe, but to see how simple and approachable a creative life is. It's not about adding layers to your life, but about stripping away obstacles. Fear is one of the biggest obstacles any of us can face. Fear of rejection, fear of loss, fear of inadequacy. Don't allow your fears and anxieties to overshadow your passions. Life itself is an artistic expression, so you already have the capacity to create beauty. You don't have to be an expert drawer or painter, or even seamstress. You just have to bring to fruition the ideas in your life that inspire you and that will help make life better for others.

I'm very happy making my art as a designer. But the artistic energy also extends into the way we run our business and work to effect positive changes in our community and beyond. Every decision is looked at with respect to how it will affect other people. We want to improve the lives of those whom we touch. Giving back is a privilege. It's also a way of life that elevates the spirit and encourages those around you to take responsibility for and ownership of society as a whole. We can't hide behind our advantages and ignore problems until they go away. A better world is constantly maintained, not finally achieved.

Beauty is in the way you live. Enjoy your surroundings. Let them inspire you. Follow your own path, and approach everything you do with love in your heart.

-Amy

Resource Guide

I've presented a few ideas and inspirations in this book and it is my hope that you've culled a few of them for your very own. Here's a list of potential resources for you to discover new ideas, objects, and information.

Amy's Website

www.amybutlerdesign.com
FASHION, HOME, & INSPIRATION

Home Decor

www.anthropologie.com
GREAT FASHION AND HOME DECOR

www.abchome.com
A VARIETY OF GREAT HOME DECOR

www.dwr.com
MODERN FURNITURE & ACCESSORIES

www.plushpod.com
MODERN FURNITURE & ACCESSORIES

www.2modern.com
MODERN FURNITURE & ACCESSORIES

www.hivemodern.com
MODERN FURNITURE & ACCESSORIES

www.designpublic.com
MODERN FURNITURE & ACCESSORIES

www.crateandbarrel.com
FURNITURE & ACCESSORIES

www.roomandboard.com
FURNITURE & ACCESSORIES

www.ikea.com
FURNITURE & ACCESSORIES

www.modernethnic.com
PRIMITIVE FURNITURE DESIGNS

www.johnderian.com
A VARIETY OF GREAT HOME DECOR

www.greenergrassdesign.com
A VARIETY OF GREAT HOME DECOR

www.thehomeport.com
A VARIETY OF GREAT HOME DECOR

www.publicliving.com
A VARIETY OF GREAT HOME DECOR

www.americanfurnishings.com
CLASSIC & MODERN FURNISHINGS

www.ochre.net
A VARIETY OF GREAT HOME DECOR

www.urbanoutfitters.com
AFFORDABLE URBAN HOME WARES

www.fishseddy.com
VINTAGE DINNERWARE

www.mikasa.com
AMY'S DINNERWARE

Antiques

www.antiqueshopsa2z.com
ANTIQUE SHOPS FINDER

www.antique-shop.com
ANTIQUE SHOPS FINDER

www.curioscape.com
ANTIQUE SHOPS FINDER

www.sonrisafurniture.com
VINTAGE MODERN HOME & OFFICE

Antique Shows

www.brimfieldshow.com
BRIMFIELD, MA

www.jenkinsshows.com
SPRINGFIELD, OH

www.roundtop-marburger.com
ROUND TOP, TX

www.vintagefashionandtextiles.com
STURBRIDGE, MA

www.quilts.com
INTERNATIONAL QUILT FESTIVAL

Fashion

www.revolveclothing.com
HUGE LIST OF DESIGNER FASHIONS

www.hm.com
AFFORDABLE FASHIONS

www.scoopnyc.com
DESIGNER FASHIONS

www.zappos.com
ENDLESS SHOES

www.patagonia.com
ACTIVEWEAR WITH A CONSCIENCE

www.stewartbrown.com
BEAUTIFUL ORGANIC CLOTHING

www.kim-metteedesigns.com
AMAZING HANDMADE JEWELRY

www.granvillemillinerycompany.com
GORGEOUS HAND-MADE HATS

Great Style Blogs

www.decor8.com
SHARE YOUR PROJECTS!

www.lifever.coxi.org
INSPIRED FASHION AND HOME DECOR

www.dailycandy.com
STAY UP-TO-DATE ON COOL FINDS

www.stylebakery.com
FUN FASHION AND SHOPPING

www.apartmenttherapy.com
GROOVY HOME IDEAS / TIPS / SHOPPING

www.mocoloco.com
COOL MODERN DESIGN

www.urbanprarie.net
ALTERNATIVE COUNTRY STYLE

FABRICS

www.amybutlerdesign.com/buy
A LISTING OF THE BEST
FABRIC RETAILERS ANYWHERE

www.westminsterfibers.com
HOME OF AMY'S FABRICS ALONGSIDE
MANY OTHER AMAZING ARTISTS

www.reprodepotfabrics.com
VINTAGE & MODERN STYLES

www.poly-fil.com
FAIRFIELD -MAKERS OF
ENVIRONMENTALLY FRIENDLY
NATURE-FIL AND NU-FOAM

www.purlsoho.com
SUPERCOOL SEWING AND KNITTING SHOP

www.frenchgeneral.com
NOTIONS, TRIMS, & TEXTILES

www.onboardfabrics.com
UNIQUE IMPORTED FABRICS

www.salsafabrics.com
UNIQUE IMPORTED FABRICS

www.harmonyart.com
BEAUTIFUL ORGANIC FABRICS

FOOD / KITCHEN

www.herbs-teas.com
MOOTZ RUN EXOTIC TEAS

www.templespice.com
FRESH, EXOTIC SPICES

www.williamsonoma.com
WONDERFUL FOODS & KITCHENWARE

www.deandeluca.com
WONDERFUL FOODS & KITCHENWARE

www.wasserstromcompany.com
RESTAURANT SUPPLY - STAINLESS STEEL

www.galley.com
RESTAURANT SUPPLY - STAINLESS STEEL

PLANTS/FLOWERS/GARDEN

www.firmlyplanted.net
STUNNING CONTAINER COMBINATIONS

www.bloomsdirect.com
CUT FLOWERS FOR THE HOME

www.agrotropical.andes.com
TROPICAL FLOWERS DÉLIVERED

www.plantdelights.com
TROPICALS & PERENNIALS

www.rootsrhizomes.com
DAYLILLIES, HOSTAS, IRIS, PERENNIALS

www.songsparrow.com
RARE & SPECIAL PERENNIALS

www.heronswood.com
GORGEOUS PERENNIALS

www.mzbulb.com
QUALITY BULBS

www.smithandhawken.com
PLANTS, ACCESSORIES, SUPPLIES

www.leevalley.com
GREAT GARDENING SUPPLIES

www.nettletonhollow.com
INCREDIBLE DRIED PLANTS

CREATIVE TIME

www.kandcompany.com
AMY'S PAPER CRAFTS & SCRAPBOOKING

www.janome.com
THE SEWING MACHINE AMY USES

www.craftyplanet.com
SUPERCOOL SEWING AND KNITTING SHOP

www.utrecht.com
GREAT ART SUPPLIES

www.dickblick.com
GREAT ART SUPPLIES

GREEN LIVING

www.thegreenguide.com
GREEN LIVING GUIDE

www.newdream.org
CONCIOUS CONSUMER TIPS

www.organicconsumers.org
REFERENCE FOR ORGANIC BUYING

www.naturalhighlifestyle.com
NATURAL CLOTHING AND HOME

www.ams.usda.gov/farmersmarkets
REFERENCE LIST FOR LOCAL MARKETS

GIVING BACK

www.youthfortechnology.org
COMPUTERS FOR DISADVANTAGED AREAS

www.redshield.org
DONTATE TO THE SALVATION ARMY

www.onewarmcoat.org
FREE COATS FOR THOSE IN NEED

www.suitcasesforkids.org
SUITCASES FOR FOSTER CHILDREN

www.cap4pets.com
CITIZENS FOR ANIMAL PROTECTION

www.habitat.org
HABITAT FOR HUMANITY

www.coopamerica.org
ECONOMIC ACTION FOR A JUST PLANET

WHERE WE SHOP LOCALLY

www.farleyandmooreantiques.com
ANTIQUES

www.collierwest.com
MOD HOME FURNISHINGS

www.sobostyle.com
COUNTRY HOME FURNISHINGS

www.mygreenvelvet.com
HOME FURNISHINGS & FASHION